JavaScript for Web Development

Master the Art of Building Dynamic and Interactive Web Applications

A Comprehensive Guide

Written by: Joseph Martin

Contents

Introduction of the book

Introduction: "JavaScript for Web Development"

Welcome to "JavaScript for Web Development," a comprehensive guide that will equip you with the knowledge and skills to harness the power of JavaScript in building robust and interactive web applications. In this book, we will delve into the world of JavaScript, exploring its fundamental concepts, practical techniques, and best practices.

JavaScript has become an essential programming language for web development, enabling developers to create dynamic and engaging user experiences. From client-side interactivity to server-side scripting, JavaScript plays a pivotal role in modern web development.

In this book, we will start by laying a solid foundation in JavaScript, covering core concepts such as variables, data types, control structures, functions, and object-oriented programming. We'll explore how JavaScript interacts with HTML and CSS, enabling you to manipulate the Document Object Model (DOM), handle events, and create dynamic web pages.

As we progress, we'll dive deeper into advanced JavaScript topics, including asynchronous programming with Promises and async/await, working with APIs to fetch data, and leveraging modern ES6+ features to write cleaner and more efficient code. Additionally, we'll cover essential topics like error handling, debugging techniques, performance optimization, security best practices, deployment strategies, and local development environments. These aspects are crucial for ensuring the reliability, efficiency, and security of your web applications. Throughout this book, you'll find hands-on examples, code snippets, and practical projects that will solidify your understanding of JavaScript concepts and provide real-world applications. You'll gain the confidence to write clean and maintainable code, troubleshoot issues effectively, and build robust and feature-rich web applications.

Whether you're a beginner taking your first steps into web development or an experienced developer looking to enhance your JavaScript skills, "JavaScript for Web Development" is your comprehensive guide. By the end of this book, you'll have the knowledge and confidence to create dynamic and interactive web applications that will delight users and make your mark in the ever-evolving world of web development.

So, let's embark on this exciting journey together and unlock the full potential of JavaScript for web development!

Chapter 1

Introduction to JavaScript

Section 1.1: Overview of JavaScript and its Role in Web Development

JavaScript is a versatile programming language that plays a crucial role in web development. It enables developers to create interactive and dynamic elements on web pages, enhancing the overall user experience. In this section, we'll explore the fundamental concepts of JavaScript and its significance in web development, providing easy-to-understand explanations and practical examples.

1.1.1 What is JavaScript?

JavaScript is a high-level, interpreted programming language that runs on the client side (in the user's web browser) as well as the server side. It is primarily used for web development, allowing developers to create interactive and responsive websites. Unlike HTML and CSS, which focus on the structure and presentation of web content, JavaScript adds functionality and interactivity to web pages.

Example 1.1.1: Adding JavaScript to HTML

```
<!DOCTYPE html>

<html>

<head>

<title>JavaScript Example</title>

<script>

// JavaScript code goes here

alert('Hello, JavaScript!');

</script>

</head>

<body>

<h1>Welcome to my website!</h1>

</body>

</html>
```

1.1.2 JavaScript in Web Development

JavaScript is widely used in web development due to its ability to enhance interactivity and provide a dynamic user experience. It allows developers to respond to user actions, manipulate web page elements, make HTTP requests, and perform calculations, among many other tasks. Additionally,

JavaScript frameworks and libraries, such as React, Angular, and jQuery, provide powerful tools and abstractions that simplify web development.

Example 1.1.2: Changing Element Content

```html
<!DOCTYPE html>

<html>

<head>

<title>JavaScript Example</title>

<script>

function changeText() {

document.getElementById('demo').innerHTML = 'Hello, JavaScript!';

}

</script>

</head>

<body>

<h1 id="demo">Welcome</h1>

<button onclick="changeText()">Click me</button>

</body>

</html>
```

In the above example, a JavaScript function changeText() is defined. When the button is clicked, the function is called, and it changes the content of the <h1> element to "Hello, JavaScript!".

JavaScript's popularity in the web development industry continues to grow, making it an essential skill for developers to master. In the following chapters, we will explore JavaScript in-depth, covering its syntax, data types, control flow, and other crucial concepts that will empower you to build dynamic and interactive web applications.

Chapter 2

Variables and Data Types

Section 2.1: Introduction to Variables

Variables are fundamental elements in programming that allow us to store and manipulate data. In this section, we'll explore variables in JavaScript, how to declare and initialize them, and their role in web development. We'll provide easy-to-understand explanations and practical examples to help you grasp the concept of variables effectively.

2.1.1 Declaring Variables

Variables in JavaScript are declared using the var, let, or const keyword, followed by the variable name. The var keyword is the traditional way of declaring variables, while let and const are introduced in newer versions of JavaScript.

Example 2.1.1: Variable Declaration

var message;

let count;

const PI = 3.14159;

In the above example, we declared three variables: message, count, and PI. The var and let keywords are used for variables whose values can be reassigned, while const is used for variables that should remain constant throughout the program.

2.1.2 Initializing Variables

Variables can be initialized with an initial value at the time of declaration. Initialization is done using the assignment operator (=).

Example 2.1.2: Variable Initialization

var name = "John";

let age = 25;

const isAdult = true;

In the above example, we declared and initialized three variables: name, age, and isAdult. The variables name and age are assigned string and number values, respectively, while the variable isAdult is assigned a boolean value.

Section 2.2: Data Types in JavaScript

JavaScript supports several data types, including strings, numbers, booleans, arrays, objects, and more. Understanding these data types is essential as they determine how data is stored and processed in JavaScript.

2.2.1 Strings

Strings are used to represent textual data in JavaScript. They are enclosed in single quotes ('...') or double quotes ("...").

Example 2.2.1: String Variables

var message = "Hello, JavaScript!";

let name = 'John';

const greeting = "Welcome to our website";

In the above example, we have assigned string values to the variables message, name, and greeting.

2.2.2 Numbers

Numbers in JavaScript can be integers or floating-point values.

Example 2.2.2: Number Variables

var count = 10;

let price = 99.99;

const pi = 3.14;

In the above example, we have assigned number values to the variables count, price, and pi.

2.2.3 Booleans

Booleans represent a logical value of either true or false. They are commonly used in conditional statements and comparisons.

Example 2.2.3: Boolean Variables

var isLogged = true;

let isActive = false;

const isAdmin = true;

In the above example, we have assigned boolean values to the variables isLogged, isActive, and isAdmin.

These are just a few of the basic data types in JavaScript. In later chapters, we'll explore more complex data types like arrays and objects.

Understanding the different data types is crucial as it enables you to manipulate and work with data effectively in your web development projects.

Chapter 3

Control Flow and Looping

Section 3.1: Conditional Statements

In this section, we'll dive into conditional statements in JavaScript. Conditional statements allow us to make decisions and execute different blocks of code based on certain conditions. Understanding conditional statements is essential for controlling the flow of execution in our programs.

3.1.1 if Statement

The if statement is the most basic conditional statement in JavaScript. It allows us to execute a block of code only if a specific condition is true.

Example 3.1.1: Using the if Statement

```
var age = 18;

if (age >= 18) {

console.log("You are an adult.");

}
```

In the above example, we use the if statement to check if the age variable is greater than or equal to 18. If the condition evaluates to true, the message "You are an adult." will be logged to the console.

3.1.2 if...else Statement

The if...else statement expands upon the if statement by providing an alternative block of code to execute when the condition is false.

Example 3.1.2: Using the if...else Statement

```
var age = 15;

if (age >= 18) {

console.log("You are an adult.");

} else {

console.log("You are not yet an adult.");

}
```

In the above example, the condition age >= 18 is evaluated. If the condition is true, the message "You are an adult." is logged. Otherwise, the message "You are not yet an adult." is logged.

3.1.3 else if Statement

The else if statement allows us to check multiple conditions in a sequence. It is useful when we have more than two possible outcomes.

Example 3.1.3: Using the else if Statement

```
var time = 14;

if (time < 12) {

console.log("Good morning!");

} else if (time < 18) {

console.log("Good afternoon!");

} else {

console.log("Good evening!");

}
```

In the above example, we check the value of the time variable. Depending on its value, different messages are logged to the console.

Section 3.2: Iteration and Looping

This section focuses on iteration and looping structures in JavaScript. Loops allow us to repeatedly execute a block of code, making them useful when dealing with repetitive tasks or working with collections of data.

3.2.1 for Loop

The for loop is a commonly used loop structure in JavaScript. It allows us to execute a block of code for a specified number of iterations.

Example 3.2.1: Using the for Loop

```
for (var i = 1; i <= 5; i++) {

console.log("Iteration: " + i);

}
```

In the above example, the for loop is used to iterate from 1 to 5. The loop will execute the code block inside it for each iteration, logging the iteration number to the console

3.2.2 while Loop

The while loop continues to execute a block of code as long as a specified condition remains true.

Example 3.2.2: Using the while Loop

```
var count = 1;

while (count <= 5) {

console.log("Count: " + count);

count++;

}
```

In the above example, the while loop is used to iterate and log the value of the count variable as long as it is less than or equal to 5.

3.2.3 do...while Loop

The do...while loop is similar to the while loop but with a slight difference. It executes the code block first and then checks the condition. This guarantees that the code block executes at least once.

Example 3.2.3: Using the do...while Loop

var x = 1;

do {

console.log("Value of x: " + x);

x++;

} while (x <= 5);

In the above example, the do...while loop is used to log the value of x and increment it. The loop will continue executing as long as x is less than or equal to 5.

Understanding conditional statements and looping structures allows you to create dynamic and responsive code. By controlling the flow and repeating tasks, you can build powerful web applications. In the following chapters, we'll explore more advanced concepts and techniques that will further enhance your JavaScript skills.

Chapter 4

Functions

Section 4.1: Introduction to Functions

Functions are essential building blocks in JavaScript that allow us to organize and reuse code. In this section, we'll explore functions in detail, their syntax, and their role in web development. Understanding functions is crucial for writing modular and maintainable code.

4.1.1 Function Definition

A function in JavaScript is a reusable block of code that performs a specific task. It takes input values (arguments) and returns an output value, if needed. Functions are defined using the function keyword, followed by the function name, parentheses for arguments, and a block of code enclosed in curly braces.

Example 4.1.1: Function Definition

```
function greet() {

console.log("Hello, World!");

}
```

In the above example, we define a function named greet that logs the message "Hello, World!" to the console.

4.1.2 Function Invocation

To execute a function and run its code, we need to invoke or call the function. Function invocation is done by using the function name followed by parentheses.

Example 4.1.2: Function Invocation

greet(); // Output: Hello, World!

In the above example, we invoke the greet function, causing it to execute and log the message to the console.

Section 4.2: Function Parameters and Return Values

In this section, we'll explore function parameters and return values. Parameters allow us to pass values into functions, and return values enable functions to provide output back to the caller.

4.2.1 Function Parameters

Parameters are placeholders for values that we can pass to a function when invoking it. They allow functions to accept inputs and perform operations on them. Parameters are defined within the parentheses of the function declaration.

Example 4.2.1: Function with Parameters

function greet(name) {

console.log("Hello, " + name + "!");

greet("John"); // Output: Hello, John!

In the above example, the greet function takes a name parameter and logs a personalized greeting to the console based on the provided name.

4.2.2 Return Values

Functions can also return values using the return statement. The returned value can be assigned to a variable or used directly in further calculations.

Example 4.2.2: Function with Return Value

```
function square(number) {

return number * number;

}

var result = square(5);

console.log(result); // Output: 25
```

In the above example, the square function accepts a number parameter and returns the square of that number. The returned value is stored in the variable result and then logged to the console.

Section 4.3: Function Scope and Closures

In this section, we'll explore function scope and closures, which determine the accessibility of variables within functions.

4.3.1 Function Scope

JavaScript has function scope, which means variables declared within a function are only accessible within that function. Variables declared outside of any function have global scope and can be accessed throughout the code.

Example 4.3.1: Function Scope

```
function myFunction() {

var message = "Hello";

console.log(message); // Output: Hello

}

myFunction();

console.log(message); // Output: ReferenceError: message is not defined
```

In the above example, the message variable is declared within the myFunction function and can only be accessed within that function. Trying to access the message variable outside the function results in a ReferenceError.

4.3.2 Closures

Closures are a powerful feature in JavaScript that allows functions to retain access to variables from the outer (enclosing) scope, even after the outer function has finished executing.

Example 4.3.2: Closures

```
function outerFunction() {

var message = "Hello";

function innerFunction() {

console.log(message);

}

return innerFunction;
```

```
}
```

var closure = outerFunction();

closure(); // Output: Hello

In the above example, the outerFunction defines an innerFunction that has access to the message variable from its enclosing scope. The outerFunction returns the innerFunction, which is then assigned to the variable closure. When closure is invoked, it still has access to the message variable and logs its value.

Understanding functions, their parameters, return values, scope, and closures will greatly enhance your ability to write efficient and reusable code. Functions play a vital role in web development by encapsulating functionality and promoting code organization. In the upcoming chapters, we'll delve deeper into more advanced JavaScript concepts and techniques.

Chapter 5

Arrays and Objects

Section 5.1: Arrays

Arrays are versatile data structures that allow us to store and manipulate multiple values in a single variable. In this section, we'll explore arrays in JavaScript, their properties, methods, and practical examples.

5.1.1 Creating Arrays

Arrays in JavaScript are created using square brackets [] and can contain any combination of values, including numbers, strings, booleans, objects, and even other arrays.

Example 5.1.1: Creating an Array

var fruits = ["apple", "banana", "orange"];

In the above example, we create an array named fruits that contains three string values.

5.1.2 Accessing Array Elements

Individual elements in an array are accessed using their index, which starts at 0. We can use square brackets [] with the index to retrieve or modify the value of a specific element.

Example 5.1.2: Accessing Array Elements

```
var fruits = ["apple", "banana", "orange"];
console.log(fruits[0]); // Output: apple
console.log(fruits[1]); // Output: banana
```

```
fruits[2] = "grape"; // Modifying the value at index 2
console.log(fruits[2]); // Output: grape
```

In the above example, we access and log the values of the elements at index 0 and index 1 of the fruits array. We also modify the value at index 2 and log the updated value.

5.1.3 Array Methods

Arrays come with a variety of built-in methods that allow us to manipulate and perform operations on array elements. Some commonly used methods include push, pop, length, splice, and forEach.

Example 5.1.3: Array Methods

```
var fruits = ["apple", "banana", "orange"];
fruits.push("grape"); // Adds a new element to the end of the array
console.log(fruits); // Output: ["apple", "banana", "orange", "grape"]
var removedFruit = fruits.pop(); // Removes the last element and returns it
```

```
console.log(removedFruit); // Output: grape
```

```
console.log(fruits.length); // Output: 3
```

```
fruits.splice(1, 1, "kiwi"); // Removes one element at index 1 and adds
"kiwi" in its place
```

```
console.log(fruits); // Output: ["apple", "kiwi", "orange"]
```

In the above example, we demonstrate some commonly used array methods. We add an element to the end of the array using push, remove the last element and store it in a variable using pop, retrieve the length of the array using length, and replace an element using splice.

Section 5.2: Objects

Objects are fundamental in JavaScript and allow us to store and manipulate complex data structures. In this section, we'll explore objects, their properties, methods, and practical examples.

5.2.1 Creating Objects

Objects in JavaScript are created using curly braces {} and consist of key-value pairs. Keys are also known as properties, and their associated values can be of any data type.

Example 5.2.1: Creating an Object

```
var person = {

name: "John",

age: 25,

isStudent: true

};
```

In the above example, we create an object named person with properties such as name, age, and isStudent.

5.2.2 Accessing Object Properties

Object properties are accessed using dot notation (object.property) or bracket notation (object['property']).

Example 5.2.2: Accessing Object Properties

```
var person = {

name: "John",

age: 25,

isStudent: true

};

console.log(person.name); // Output: John

console.log(person['age']); // Output: 25
```

In the above example, we access and log the values of the name property using dot notation and the age property using bracket notation.

5.2.3 Object Methods

Objects can also have methods, which are functions defined as properties of the object. Methods allow objects to perform actions or calculations.

Example 5.2.3: Object Methods

```
var person = {

name: "John",

age: 25,

isStudent: true,

greet: function() {

console.log("Hello, my name is " + this.name + ".");

}

};

person.greet(); // Output: Hello, my name is John.
```

In the above example, we define a greet method as a property of the person object. The method logs a greeting message that includes the person's name using the this keyword to refer to the object's own property.

Understanding arrays and objects is crucial for working with complex data structures and organizing information in web development. Arrays allow us to store and manipulate multiple values efficiently, while objects provide a way to represent and work with more complex entities. In the upcoming chapters, we'll explore advanced concepts and techniques that will further enhance your JavaScript skills.

Chapter 6

DOM Manipulation

Section 6.1: Introduction to the DOM

The Document Object Model (DOM) is a programming interface for web documents. It represents the structure and content of an HTML or XML document as a tree-like structure, where each element, attribute, and text node is represented as an object. In this chapter, we'll explore DOM manipulation using JavaScript, allowing us to dynamically update and interact with web pages.

6.1.1 Accessing DOM Elements

To access and manipulate elements in the DOM, we use JavaScript methods and properties. The document object represents the entire document, and from there, we can navigate and interact with various elements.

Example 6.1.1: Accessing DOM Elements

// Accessing an element by its ID

var heading = document.getElementById('my-heading');

// Accessing elements by their class name

var paragraphs = document.getElementsByClassName('my-paragraph');

```
// Accessing elements by their tag name
```

```
var links = document.getElementsByTagName('a');
```

In the above example, we use different methods to access DOM elements. We access an element by its ID using getElementById, elements by their class name using getElementsByClassName, and elements by their tag name using getElementsByTagName.

6.1.2 Modifying DOM Elements

Once we have accessed a DOM element, we can modify its properties, attributes, and content using JavaScript.

Example 6.1.2: Modifying DOM Elements

```
var heading = document.getElementById('my-heading');
```

```
// Modifying the text content
```

```
heading.textContent = 'New Heading';
```

```
// Modifying the CSS class
```

```
heading.classList.add('highlight');
```

```
// Modifying an attribute
```

```
heading.setAttribute('data-custom', 'value');
```

In the above example, we modify the text content of an element using the textContent property, add a CSS class using the classList property and the add method, and modify an attribute using the setAttribute method.

Section 6.2: Event Handling

Event handling allows us to respond to user interactions or other events triggered on web pages. We can use JavaScript to attach event listeners to DOM elements and execute code when specific events occur.

6.2.1 Adding Event Listeners

Event listeners are functions that are executed when a specific event occurs on an element. We can use the addEventListener method to attach event listeners to DOM elements.

Example 6.2.1: Adding Event Listeners

```
var button = document.getElementById('my-button');

button.addEventListener('click', function() {

// Code to execute when the button is clicked

console.log('Button clicked!');

});
```

In the above example, we attach an event listener to a button element that listens for the 'click' event. When the button is clicked, the provided function is executed.

6.2.2 Event Object

When an event occurs, additional information about the event is passed to the event listener function through the event object. This object contains useful properties and methods related to the event.

Example 6.2.2: Event Object

```javascript
var button = document.getElementById('my-button');

button.addEventListener('click', function(event) {

// Accessing event properties

console.log('Button clicked at coordinates:', event.clientX, event.clientY);

});
```

In the above example, we access the clientX and clientY properties of the event object to log the coordinates of the mouse click.

Understanding DOM manipulation and event handling allows us to create dynamic and interactive web pages. With JavaScript, we can access, modify, and respond to elements and events, providing a richer user experience. In the next chapters, we'll explore more advanced techniques and concepts in web development using JavaScript.

Chapter 7

Asynchronous JavaScript

Section 7.1: Introduction to Asynchronous Programming

Asynchronous programming is a fundamental concept in JavaScript that allows us to handle tasks that may take time to complete without blocking the execution of other code. In this chapter, we'll explore asynchronous JavaScript, including callbacks, promises, and async/await, which are essential for dealing with time-consuming operations, such as fetching data from servers or handling user interactions.

7.1.1 Understanding Asynchronous Behavior

In JavaScript, code is executed sequentially by default, meaning that each line of code is executed one after another. However, certain operations, like making an API call or reading a file, can take a significant amount of time. Asynchronous programming allows us to handle these tasks without blocking the execution of other code.

7.1.2 Callback Functions

Callback functions are a common approach to handle asynchronous operations in JavaScript. A callback function is a function that is passed as an argument to another function and is called when a specific task is completed.

Example 7.1.2: Using a Callback Function

```javascript
function fetchData(callback) {

// Simulating an asynchronous task

setTimeout(function() {

var data = 'Fetched data';

callback(data);

}, 2000);

}

function handleData(data) {

console.log('Received data:', data);

}

fetchData(handleData);
```

In the above example, the fetchData function simulates an asynchronous task using setTimeout. After the task is completed, it calls the provided callback function handleData and passes the fetched data as an argument.

Section 7.2: Promises

Promises are a modern approach to handle asynchronous operations in JavaScript. A promise is an object that represents the eventual completion (or failure) of an asynchronous task and allows us to attach callbacks to handle the result.

7.2.1 Creating Promises

Promises are created using the Promise constructor and take a function as an argument. This function, called the executor, contains the asynchronous task that eventually resolves or rejects the promise

Example 7.2.1: Creating a Promise

```
function fetchData() {

return new Promise(function(resolve, reject) {

// Simulating an asynchronous task

setTimeout(function() {

var data = 'Fetched data';

resolve(data);

}, 2000);

});

}

fetchData()

.then(function(data) {

console.log('Received data:', data);

})

.catch(function(error) {

console.log('Error:', error);

});
```

In the above example, the fetchData function returns a promise that wraps the asynchronous task. The promise is resolved with the fetched data using the resolve function, and any errors are rejected using the reject function. We can use the then method to handle the resolved data and the catch method to handle any errors.

7.2.2 Chaining Promises

Promises can be chained together to handle multiple asynchronous operations in a sequential manner. Each then method returns a new promise, allowing us to perform subsequent operations.

Example 7.2.2: Chaining Promises

```
function fetchData() {

return new Promise(function(resolve, reject) {

// Simulating an asynchronous task

setTimeout(function() {

var data = 'Fetched data';

resolve(data);

}, 2000);

});

}

function processData(data) {

return new Promise(function(resolve, reject) {

// Simulating an asynchronous task
```

```
setTimeout(function() {

var processedData = data.toUpperCase();

resolve(processedData);

}, 1000);

});

}

fetchData()

.then(processData)

.then(function(result) {

console.log('Processed data:', result);

})

.catch(function(error) {

console.log('Error:', error);

});
```

In the above example, we chain promises by returning a new promise from the then method. The processData function receives the resolved data, performs some processing, and returns a new promise. The final then method receives the processed result and logs it.

Section 7.3: Async/Await

Async/await is a modern syntax for handling asynchronous operations in JavaScript. It provides a more concise and readable way to write asynchronous code, using the async and await keywords.

7.3.1 Defining Async Functions

An async function is a function that returns a promise and allows the usage of the await keyword to pause the execution until a promise is resolved.

Example 7.3.1: Defining an Async Function

```
async function fetchData() {

return new Promise(function(resolve, reject) {

// Simulating an asynchronous task

setTimeout(function() {

var data = 'Fetched data';

resolve(data);

}, 2000);

});

}

async function processData() {

var data = await fetchData();

var processedData = data.toUpperCase();

return processedData;

}

processData()

.then(function(result) {
```

```javascript
console.log('Processed data:', result);
})
.catch(function(error) {
console.log('Error:', error);
});
```

In the above example, the fetchData function returns a promise, and the processData function uses the await keyword to pause the execution until the promise is resolved. The await keyword allows us to assign the resolved value to the data variable and perform further processing.

Understanding asynchronous JavaScript is essential for handling time-consuming operations and creating responsive web applications. Whether using callback functions, promises, or async/await, asynchronous programming allows us to efficiently handle tasks without blocking the execution of other code. In the next chapters, we'll explore more advanced topics and techniques in JavaScript web development.

Chapter 8

Working with APIs

Section 8.1: Introduction to APIs

Application Programming Interfaces (APIs) allow different software systems to communicate and exchange data with each other. In web development, APIs play a crucial role in fetching data from external sources, such as remote servers, and integrating that data into web applications. In this chapter, we'll explore how to work with APIs using JavaScript.

8.1.1 Understanding API Basics

APIs define a set of rules and protocols for how software components should interact. They provide a structured way to request and receive data from a server or external service. APIs can return data in various formats, such as JSON or XML, which can be easily parsed and used in web applications.

8.1.2 Making HTTP Requests

To interact with an API, we use HTTP requests. JavaScript provides several methods and libraries for making HTTP requests, such as the fetch API and popular libraries like Axios and jQuery.

Example 8.1.2: Making an HTTP Request with fetch

```
fetch('https://api.example.com/data')

.then(function(response) {

return response.json();

})

.then(function(data) {

console.log('Received data:', data);

})

.catch(function(error) {

console.log('Error:', error);

});
```

In the above example, we use the fetch function to make an HTTP GET request to the specified URL. We handle the response using the then method and parse the response data as JSON. Finally, we log the received data or any errors that occur.

Section 8.2: Working with JSON Data

JSON (JavaScript Object Notation) is a popular data format used for transmitting structured data between a server and a web application. It is widely supported in APIs and is easy to parse and work with in JavaScript.

8.2.1 Parsing JSON Data

To parse JSON data in JavaScript, we use the JSON.parse() method. It takes a JSON string as input and converts it into a JavaScript object.

Example 8.2.1: Parsing JSON Data

```
var jsonString = '{"name": "John", "age": 25, "isStudent": true}';

var jsonData = JSON.parse(jsonString);

console.log('Parsed data:', jsonData);
```

In the above example, we have a JSON string representing an object. We use the JSON.parse() method to convert it into a JavaScript object. The parsed object is then logged to the console.

8.2.2 Stringifying JavaScript Objects

To convert a JavaScript object into a JSON string, we use the JSON.stringify() method. It takes a JavaScript object as input and returns a JSON string.

Example 8.2.2: Stringifying JavaScript Objects

```
var data = {

name: 'John',

age: 25,

isStudent: true

};

var jsonString = JSON.stringify(data);

console.log('Stringified data:', jsonString);
```

In the above example, we have a JavaScript object data. We use the JSON.stringify() method to convert it into a JSON string. The stringified data is then logged to the console.

Section 8.3: Using APIs in Web Applications

APIs provide a wealth of data and functionality that can be integrated into web applications to enhance their features and capabilities. By leveraging APIs, we can fetch real-time data, perform data manipulation, and interact with external services.

8.3.1 Handling API Responses

When working with APIs, we need to handle the responses appropriately. This includes checking for errors, parsing the response data, and using the data in our web applications.

Example 8.3.1: Handling API Responses

```
fetch('https://api.example.com/data')

.then(function(response) {

if (!response.ok) {

throw new Error('API request failed');

}

return response.json();

})

.then(function(data) {
```

```
// Process the data and update the web application

})

.catch(function(error) {

console.log('Error:', error);

});
```

In the above example, we check if the response status is not "ok" using the response.ok property. If an error occurs, we throw a new error object. Otherwise, we proceed to parse the response data and process it further.

8.3.2 Authenticating with APIs

Some APIs require authentication to access protected resources or perform specific actions. Authentication methods can vary, but common approaches include using API keys, OAuth, or tokens.

Example 8.3.2: Authenticating with an API

```
var apiKey = 'YOUR_API_KEY';


fetch('https://api.example.com/data', {

headers: {

'Authorization': 'Bearer ' + apiKey

}

})

.then(function(response) {
```

```
return response.json();

})

.then(function(data) {

// Process the authenticated data

})

.catch(function(error) {

console.log('Error:', error);

});
```

In the above example, we include the API key in the request headers using the Authorization field. The specific method and header format may vary depending on the API's authentication requirements.

Working with APIs allows web developers to access and utilize external data and services, making web applications more powerful and versatile. Understanding how to make HTTP requests, parse JSON data, and handle API responses is essential for integrating APIs effectively. In the next chapters, we'll dive deeper into specific API-related topics and explore practical examples.

Chapter 9

Testing and Debugging in JavaScript

Section 10.1: Importance of Testing and Debugging

Testing and debugging are essential aspects of JavaScript web development. They ensure the reliability, correctness, and performance of web applications. In this chapter, we'll discuss various testing and debugging techniques and tools to help you identify and fix issues in your JavaScript code.

10.1.1 Benefits of Testing

Identifying Bugs: Tests help uncover bugs and issues in your code by executing different scenarios and verifying expected outcomes.

Preventing Regression: Tests ensure that existing functionalities continue to work as expected when making changes or adding new features.

Maintainability: Tests provide documentation and examples of how your code should behave, making it easier for other developers to understand and work with your codebase.

Confidence: Having a comprehensive test suite gives confidence in the stability and reliability of your application.

10.1.2 Importance of Debugging Identifying Issues: Debugging helps pinpoint the root cause of issues by stepping through code and inspecting variables, values, and execution flow.

Fixing Errors: Debugging allows you to modify code and verify the changes in real-time to resolve errors and unexpected behavior.

Optimizing Performance: Debugging helps identify performance bottlenecks and optimize code for better efficiency and speed.

Section 10.2: Testing Techniques

10.2.1 Unit Testing

Unit testing involves testing individual units, such as functions or components, in isolation. It focuses on ensuring that each unit behaves correctly and produces the expected output for different inputs and edge cases.

Example 10.2.1: Unit Testing with Jest

javascript

Copy code

```
// math.js

function add(a, b) {

return a + b;

}

module.exports = add;

// math.test.js
```

```
const add = require('./math');

test('adds two numbers correctly', () => {

expect(add(2, 3)).toBe(5);

});


test('returns NaN if any argument is not a number', () => {

expect(add(2, '3')).toBeNaN();

});
```

In the above example, we use the Jest testing framework to write unit tests for a simple add function. The tests verify that the function correctly adds two numbers and returns NaN if any argument is not a number.

10.2.2 Integration Testing

Integration testing involves testing the interaction between different components or modules of an application. It ensures that these components work together correctly and produce the expected results.

Example 10.2.2: Integration Testing with Cypress

```
// login.spec.js

describe('Login', () => {

beforeEach(() => {

cy.visit('/login');
```

```
});

it('logs in a user with valid credentials', () => {
cy.get('[data-testid="email"]').type('user@example.com');
cy.get('[data-testid="password"]').type('password');
cy.get('[data-testid="submit"]').click();
cy.url().should('include', '/dashboard');
});
it('displays an error message with invalid credentials', () => {
cy.get('[data-testid="email"]').type('invalid@example.com');
cy.get('[data-testid="password"]').type('invalid');
cy.get('[data-testid="submit"]').click();
cy.contains('Invalid credentials').should('be.visible');
});
});
```

In the above example, we use Cypress, an end-to-end testing framework, to write integration tests for a login functionality. The tests simulate user interactions and verify that the login process behaves as expected.

Conclusion

Congratulations! You have completed the journey through "JavaScript for Web Development," a comprehensive guide that has equipped you with the knowledge and skills to excel in JavaScript web development. Throughout this book, we have explored the core concepts, practical techniques, and best practices that empower you to create robust and interactive web applications.

We began by establishing a solid foundation in JavaScript, understanding variables, data types, control structures, and functions. We then dived into the world of the Document Object Model (DOM) manipulation, event handling, and dynamic web page creation. As we progressed, we delved into advanced topics such as asynchronous programming, working with APIs, modularizing code, and leveraging modern ES6+ features.

By applying the knowledge gained from this book, you now have the ability to write clean, maintainable code, troubleshoot issues effectively, and build feature-rich web applications. You have learned to harness the power of JavaScript to create dynamic user experiences and deliver impactful web solutions.

Thank you for joining us on this journey through "JavaScript for Web Development." We hope that this book has provided you with a strong foundation and sparked your passion for JavaScript web development. Now, go forth, unleash your creativity, and build amazing web applications that will captivate users and make a lasting impact in the digital landscape.

www.ingramcontent.com/pod-product-compliance
Lightning Source LLC
LaVergne TN
LVHW051624050326
832903LV00033B/4642